From Gallipoli with Love

A letter from the trenches

NEIL DOHERTY

To my Nana, Mary Cutler (Mick's sister) - N.D.

For my Grandad, George Ladewig - C.L.

Published by
Boolarong Press
1/655 Toohey Road
Salisbury Qld 4105

National Library of Australia Cataloguing-in-Publication entry

Author: Doherty, Neil, author.

Title: From Gallipoli with love : a letter from the trenches / Neil Doherty; Catherine Ladewig, Illustrator.

ISBN: 9781925046311 (paperback)

Target Audience: For primary school age.

Subjects: Levine, Michael, 1884-1915--Correspondence. World War, 1914-1918--Personal narratives, Australian. Soldiers--Australia--Correspondence. World War, 1914-1918--Campaigns--Turkey--Gallipoli Peninsula--Juvenile literature. Gallipoli Peninsula (Turkey)--History, Military--Juvenile literature.

Other Authors/Contributors: Ladewig, Catherine, Illustrator.

Dewey Number: 940.426

This book is a collaboration between Neil Doherty and Catherine Ladewig, a Graphic Designer and Illustrator. All illustrations are created with watercolour and guache.

Printed in Australia by Watson Ferguson & Company

World War I

28 July 1914 – 11 November 1918

Lest We Forget

Michael Lobwein, a shearer from Meringandan - a town near Toowoomba in South-East Queensland - enlisted in 1914 using the surname Levine. It was never recorded why he changed his name but it is assumed that his original name had a German heritage. Mick's three brothers also fought in WW1 as Lobweins.

As a Private, Michael was assigned to the 15th Battalion and landed in Anzac Cove, Gallipoli on the 25th April 1915. He had been fighting for a month when he wrote this letter to his sister living in Queensland, and died in action three days later. He was 31 years old.

Gallipoli 26 May 1915

My Dear Sister

Your welcome letter to hand dated 11th April which I received in the trenches. You can imagine how pleased I was to hear from you.

I am still alive and well, and have managed to dodge the bullets and shells so far, but I am sorry to say that some of my pals have gone – but still that is the fortune of war.

Well, Mary dear, I am not sure if this letter will pass the censor or not, but I will chance it. I can't tell you much but I will do my best.

We landed at (I will call it X......) under heavy shell fire from the enemy. We had about a mile to go in open boats from the transport to the beach.

There was only one man got wounded while my company was landing, although the shrapnel was bursting overhead and bullets were splashing in the water all around us.

Shrapnel bullets were also falling in the boats but they were mostly spent and did no damage.

One man alongside of me was hit with a shrapnel bullet. It lodged on his collar badge, doubled it up, and stopped there. It never hurt him.

That was our first taste of fire but it was nothing to what we have been through since.

I have seen some queer sights since I have been here. Can't tell you all about it now but I hope to be able to do so some day.

Being under fire is a lot different to what I expected. I expected to be scared as blazes but I am exactly the opposite.

It is just like being at a football match when things are a bit lively. It makes a fellow duck his head at the start but you soon get used to it.

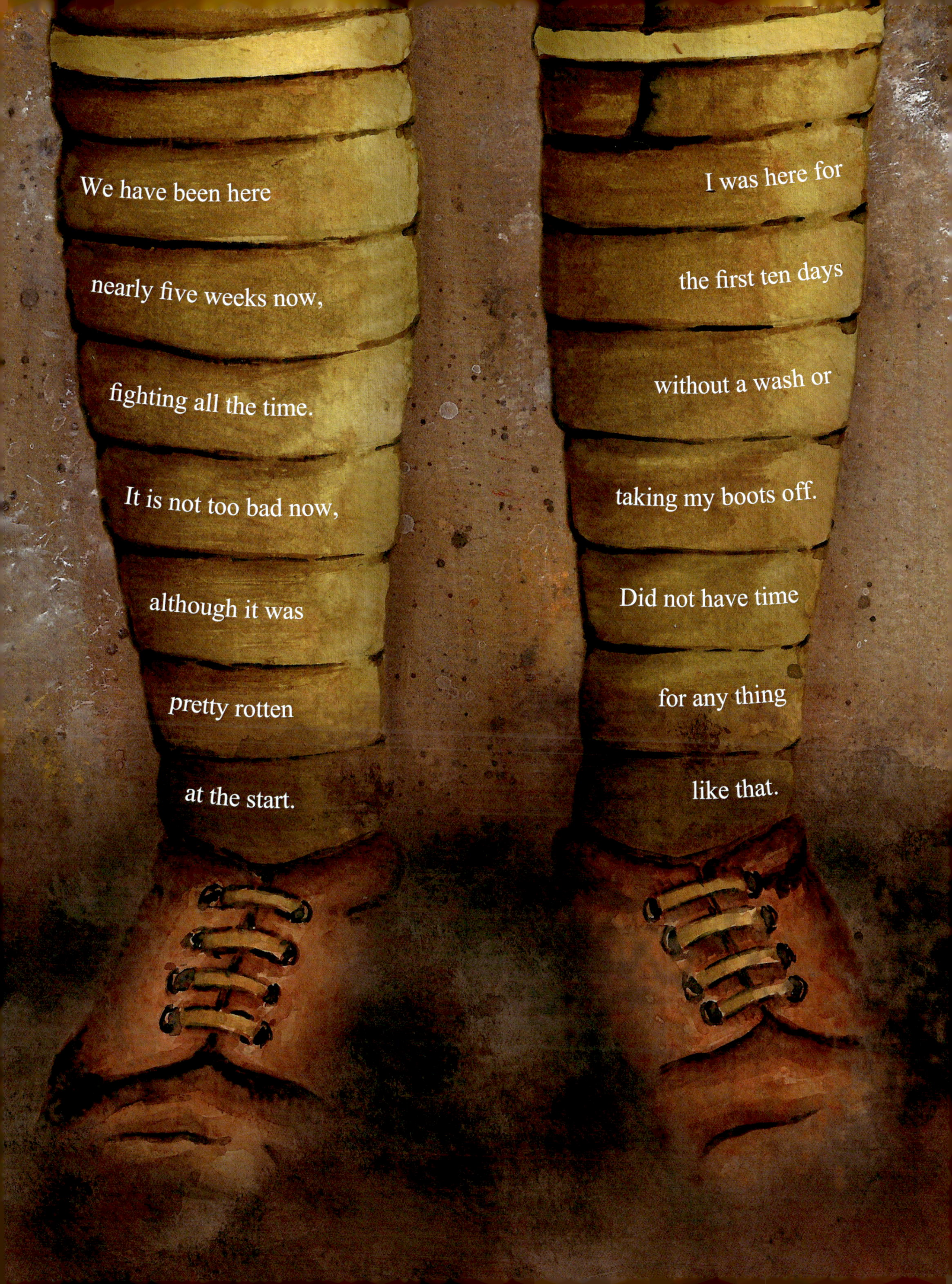

We have been here

nearly five weeks now,

fighting all the time.

It is not too bad now,

although it was

pretty rotten

at the start.

I was here for

the first ten days

without a wash or

taking my boots off.

Did not have time

for any thing

like that.

We had a rough time, but we stuck to it without a murmer, and now we hold a position which I don't think all the Turks in Gallipoli could shift us out of.

I had a thousand and one narrow escapes but, so far, have not got a scratch. Since I have been here, four men have been shot dead alongside of me and three men wounded.

I have been very lucky for, except for being half smothered with dirt and a few hits (I don't know how many) with shrapnel (spent) bullets, I am untouched.

The Turks are using explosive bullets. I have also been hit with the splinters of these.

After nearly five weeks fighting, I have come to the conclusion that this is a risky game. If they don't turn it in soon somebody will be getting hurt.

You will have to excuse this bad writing, Mary dear, as a dugout is not the best place in the world in which to write letters.

I shall never forget my first experience in the firing line. It was on the second night after landing here.

The first night I was trench digging and carrying the wounded down, which is a rotten job.

The stretcher bearers deserve great praise.

The place is very hilly and steep and covered with low undergrowth and it was wet, so you can imagine what sort of a time we had carrying the wounded down in oilsheets, blankets and stretchers.

Some of the poor beggars had been laying wounded for two days. That is the worst part of this game.

The second night we were here,
twenty men were called for to reinforce
the firing line. Well, I hopped out as
I thought I would show willing.
I had not fired a shot up till then.

Well, we went forward and there was not
enough room for all of us in the trench.
Anyhow, I was one of the unlucky ones
left out in the cold.

We had to start and dig ourselves in under heavy fire and, I can tell you, I never worked harder in my life.

All I had was a small entrenching tool, but it is marvellous how quick you can dig a hole when the bullets are flying round and ploughing up the dirt alongside of you.

The Turks advanced that night and charged our trench. They came within thirty yards of us yelling "Allah Allah" but that is as far as they got.

Well, I worked on that trench all night (in between shots) and it is just as well I did so, for, in the morning, along comes the shrapnel about daybreak. I had got down between three and four feet.

Well, it saved my life, for nothing could have lived through that storm of bullets without cover.

I was in that trench for two days when we were relieved, only to go in to the fire in another place where I remained in the trench for five days and five nights without a rest or sleep, except what you could get standing up.

This position was, if anything, hotter than the first one. All afternoon and night the Turks were advancing on our left and we got orders to keep up a continual fire.

Well, I blazed away as fast as I could load, and my rifle got that hot that I could not hold it. It was smoking and the woodwork was burning. Then I got another and, at the finish, I had three of them going turn about. I can tell you, I was pleased when that little bout was over.

I was dead beat, my hands were torn and bleeding from ramming cartridges in to the magazine. I was as deaf as a beetle - could not hear a word. My lips were cracked and throat parched but, while it was going on, I felt nothing.

Anyhow, that is all over now, but it was lively while it lasted. We work it in shifts now, 48 hours on and 72 hours off, which is not too bad.

They shall grow not old, as we that are left grow old;
Age shall not weary them, nor the years condemn.
At the going down of the sun and in the morning
We will remember them.

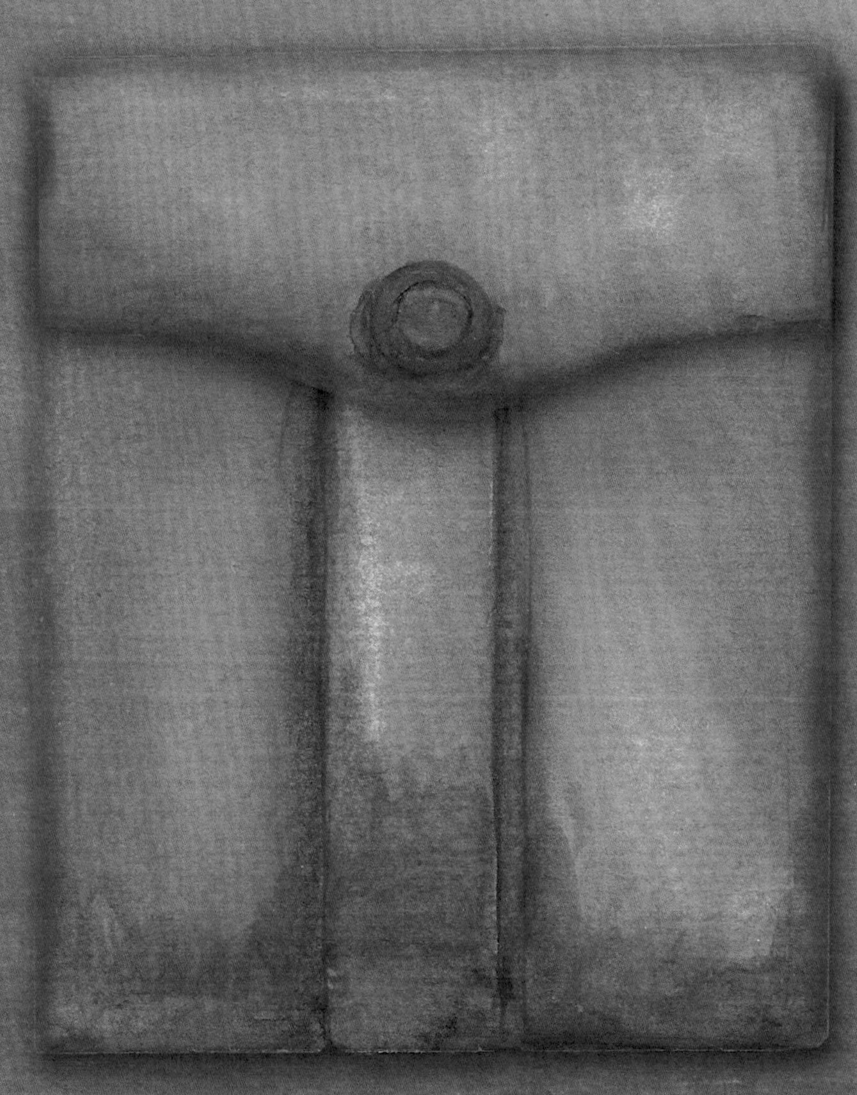

Lest We Forget